# Amazing Animals

# Tigers

Galadriel Watson

**WEIGL PUBLISHERS INC.**

Published by Weigl Publishers Inc.
350 5th Avenue, Suite 3304, PMB 6G
New York, NY 10118-0069

Amazing Animals series ©2009
WEIGL PUBLISHERS INC. www.weigl.com

Library of Congress Cataloging-in-
Publication Data

Watson, Galadriel Findlay.
  Tigers / Galadriel Watson.
    p. cm. – (Amazing animals)
  Includes index.
  ISBN 978-1-59036-962-3 (hard cover :
alk. paper) – ISBN 978-1-59036-963-0
(soft cover : alk. paper)
  1. Tigers–Juvenile literature. I. Title.
QL737.C23W377 2009
  599.756–dc22

2008003786

**Editor**
Heather Kissock
**Design and Layout**
Terry Paulhus, Kathryn Livingstone

**Photograph Credits**
Every reasonable effort has been made
to trace ownership and to obtain
permission to reprint copyright material.
The publishers would be pleased to have
any errors or omissions brought to their
attention so that they may be corrected
in subsequent printings.

All photos supplied by Getty Images.

Printed in the United States of America
1 2 3 4 5 6 7 8 9 0  12 11 10 09 08

# About This Book

This book tells you all about tigers.
Find out where they live and what
they eat. Discover how you can
help to protect them. You can
also read about them in myths
and legends from around
the world.

Words in **bold** are explained in the
Words to Know section at the back
of the book.

## Useful Websites

Addresses in this book
take you to the home pages
of websites that have
information about tigers.

All of the Internet URLs given in
the book were valid at the time
of publication. However, due to
the dynamic nature of the Internet,
some addresses may have changed,
or sites may have ceased to exist
since publication. While the
author and publisher regret any
inconvenience this may cause
readers, no responsibility for any
such changes can be accepted by
either the author or the publisher.

# Contents

# Meet the Tiger

Tigers are **mammals**. They are the biggest cats in the world. Tigers live on the continent of Asia, in countries such as India and China.

Many parts of Asia have hot, **humid** weather. During the hottest parts of the day, tigers mostly rest. They hide under trees or lie in streams or rivers. In the cool of the night, tigers become more active. This is when they hunt for food.

▼ On hot days, tigers go in the water to cool themselves.

# The Big Cats

- Tigers are closely related to other big cats, including leopards, jaguars, and lions.

- There are five types of tiger. They are the Bengal, South China, Siberian, Sumatran, and Indo-Chinese. There are also three types of tiger that are **extinct**.

▲ In nature, tigers can live to be about 15 years old.

# A Skilled Hunter

A tiger's body is built for hunting. To find **prey**, a tiger uses its great sense of hearing. It swivels its ears to locate the source of the sound. Even though it hunts at night, the tiger can see its prey. This is because the shape of its large eyes allows plenty of light to come in.

▼ A tiger can cover up to 33 feet (10 meters) in one leap.

To catch prey, a tiger relies on surprise, speed, and strength. Its claws, strong limbs, and sharp teeth help bring the prey down.

A tiger's large eyes help it see in the dark.

Great hearing allows tigers to find prey.

Striped fur helps tigers stay hidden in tall plants and grasses.

Strong jaws and sharp teeth help tigers tear and chew.

Soft pads help tigers quietly sneak up to prey.

Sharp claws come out when hunting.

Powerful limbs allow tigers to run and leap.

# Roaring

Like other big cats, tigers roar to communicate. A tiger roars in different ways. Each type of roar sends a different kind of message.

A tiger roars loudly when it has killed a large animal. This roar can be heard up to 2 miles (3 kilometers) away. A moan, or quiet roar, can be heard about 440 yards (400 m) away. It is used to attract mates. Tigers use a short, coughing roar when attacking another animal.

▶ When a tiger roars, it lays its ears back and wrinkles its nose.

## Tiger Talk

- Tigers sometimes greet each other with a snorting sound called a chuff. To chuff, a tiger closes its mouth and blows through its nose.

- Tigers also speak to one another by meowing, growling, snarling, and hissing.

# How Tigers Eat

Tigers are carnivores. This means they mostly eat other animals. They sometimes eat grass, fruits, and berries.

When hunting, a tiger tries to get as close as possible to its prey. It crouches down and moves very slowly and quietly. When the tiger gets close enough, it springs up and rushes toward the prey.

Once caught, the prey is dragged to a hiding place. The tiger will feed on the animal for several days.

▶ Few hunts are successful. It may take 10 to 20 tries before a tiger gets a kill.

# What a Meal!

- A tiger can eat up to 77 pounds (35 kilograms) of food in one feeding.

- After feeding, a tiger may not need to eat again for several days.

- A tiger hides its leftovers under leaves and sticks.

▲ Tigers are not able to chase prey very far.

# Where Tigers Live

Tigers live in all sorts of **habitats** within Asia. They can be found in forests, swamps, grasslands, mountains, and river valleys. Some of these habitats have warm, humid climates. Others have cool climates.

Tigers need to live in areas that have water sources and large prey. These areas must also offer places to hide, so tigers can sneak up on their prey. A tiger's **territory** can cover as much as 193 square miles (500 sq km).

▶ Tigers living in cool climates have a heavy fur coat.

# Tiger Range

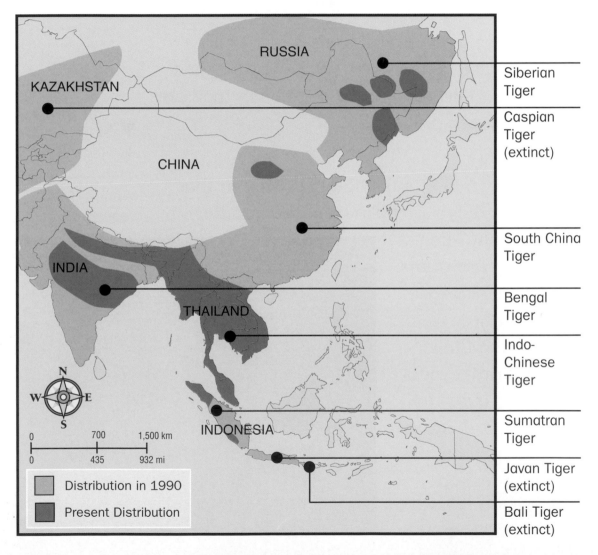

RUSSIA

KAZAKHSTAN

CHINA

INDIA

THAILAND

INDONESIA

Siberian Tiger

Caspian Tiger (extinct)

South China Tiger

Bengal Tiger

Indo-Chinese Tiger

Sumatran Tiger

Javan Tiger (extinct)

Bali Tiger (extinct)

| 0 | 700 | 1,500 km |
| 0 | 435 | 932 mi |

Distribution in 1990

Present Distribution

# Growing Up

A mother tiger gives birth to as many as four cubs at a time. These cubs are born with their eyes closed. They open their eyes when they are about one week old.

For the first two months, the cubs stay in their **den**. Then, they start following their mother to her feeding site. When they are about six months old, the cubs learn how to hunt. By the time they reach two years of age, the cubs are able to hunt their own food. They leave their mother to live on their own.

▼ A tiger's den may be in a cave, a hollow tree, or thick vegetation.

# Growth Chart

| | | |
|---|---|---|
| **Birth** | 1.7 to 3.5 pounds (0.78 to 1.6 kg) | Tiger cubs are blind and helpless. |
| **2 months old** | 22 pounds (10 kg) | Cubs begin to eat meat. |
| **6 months old** | 60 to 105 pounds (27 to 48 kg) | Cubs stop drinking their mother's milk and learn to hunt. |
| **3 to 4 years old** | 165 to 368 pounds (75 to 167 kg) | Female tigers are able to become mothers. |
| **4 to 5 years old** | 221 to 675 pounds (100 to 306 kg) | Male tigers are able to become fathers. |

▲ Tiger cubs spend much time playing. This helps them learn how to hunt.

# A Solitary Animal

Tigers are solitary animals. This means they usually live alone. Tigers form small groups only when mating or when mothers are raising their young. Most tigers avoid other tigers. A tiger may fight another tiger that comes into its territory.

Other animals stay away from tigers, too. They may become prey if they get too close.

▼ Some large animals, such as buffalo, are strong enough to injure or kill tigers.

## Useful Websites
http://animaldiversity.ummz.umich.edu

Search this website to learn more about other animals that live in the tiger's habitat.

## Living with Tigers

There are many different animals that live in the same places as tigers.

- crocodiles
- elephants
- hyenas
- leopards
- mongooses
- rhinoceroses

▼ Leopards are smaller than tigers.

# Under Threat

Humans are a tiger's greatest enemy. Some people kill tigers because they think tigers are dangerous to people and their **livestock**. Other people kill tigers to sell their fur, bones, and other body parts.

Humans are also taking away tiger habitat. They are turning these areas into towns and farms. Tigers have fewer places to live and less food to hunt.

▼ Asian governments are taking steps to stop the illegal selling of tiger skins.

## Useful Websites
http://projecttiger.nic.in

Visit this website to learn about how people are trying to help save tigers.

▲ Countries promote tigers to tourists. This brings humans directly into the tiger's natural habitat.

## What Do You Think?

Zoos help people learn about tigers. If people learn about tigers, they may want to help save them. Zoos also help increase the tiger **population**. In nature, tigers have large areas to roam. **Captive** tigers are held in much smaller spaces. Should tigers be kept in zoos? Should they be free to roam their natural habitat?

# Myths and Legends

Tigers inspire both fear and respect. Many cultures in Asia worship tigers. They believe the tiger is the king of the beasts. Some people think tigers keep away evil. Others believe tigers have magical powers.

In China, every 12th year is called the "Year of the Tiger." People born in this year are believed to be warm-hearted and strong.

During India's Onam festival, people paint their bodies like tigers. They perform a dance that tells the story of a tiger hunt.

▶ Tigers have appeared in Asian art for thousands of years.

▼ Tony the Tiger
often attends public
events, where he
can meet his fans.

## Famous Tigers

Today, books and movies often
portray tigers as friendly animals,
even though this is not true.

Tony the Tiger was first used to
sell cereal in 1951. He is known
for saying "They're Grrrreat!"

Tigger is a character in the
Winnie-the-Pooh stories. He first
showed up in the 1928 book *The
House at Pooh Corner*. The first
cartoon Tigger appeared in was
*Winnie the Pooh and the Blustery
Day*. It was made in 1968.

# Quiz

1. Where do tigers live?
   (a) **North America**  (b) **Asia**  (c) **Australia**

2. How many types of tiger live in the world today?
   (a) **three**  (b) **four**  (c) **five**

3. Which feature helps a tiger hide in plants and grasses?
   (a) **striped fur**  (b) **sharp claws**  (c) **powerful legs**

4. What other kinds of animals live near tigers?
   (a) **polar bears**  (b) **leopards**  (c) **whales**

5. When do tiger cubs first open their eyes?
   (a) **one month after being born**  (b) **at birth**
   (c) **one week after being born**

Answers:
1. (b) Tigers live in Asia.
2. (c) There are five types of tiger living in the world today.
3. (a) A tiger's striped fur helps it hide.
4. (b) Leopards live near tigers.
5. (c) Tiger cubs first open their eyes when they are about one week old.

22

# Find out More

To find out more about tigers, visit the websites in this book. You can also write to these organizations.

**Save The Tiger Fund**
**The National Fish and Wildlife Foundation**
1120 Connecticut Avenue NW, Suite 900
Washington, DC  20036

**The Tiger Foundation**
**Canada**
1055 West Georgia Street, Suite 2740
Vancouver, BC  V6E 3R5

**World Wildlife Fund**
**United States**
1250 24th Street NW
P.O. Box 97180
Washington, DC  20090-7180

# Words to Know

**captive**
the state of being confined
**den**
the hidden home of a wild animal
**extinct**
no longer living on Earth
**habitats**
the natural environments in which animals and plants live
**humid**
moist, damp
**livestock**
animals raised for food or other products

**mammals**
animals that have hair or fur and feed milk to their young
**population**
the total number of people or animals living in one place
**prey**
animals eaten by other animals
**territory**
the area that a tiger uses for hunting

# Index